DOLLARS OF LOVE

THE WHOLE WORLD IS BEAUTIFUL

By: Mikey and Elaine Hampson

Paperback ISBN 978-1-7379934-4-5

Digital ISBN 978-1-7379934-2-1

Hardcover ISBN 978-0-578-94872-0

Hello, this is Mikey and Elaine Hampson, parents to two wonderful boys and the founders of *Dollars of Love*. We wanted to tell each of you how proud we are of you for opening this book and taking the first step toward changing how the youth of today view the meaning of becoming rich.

In this book, you will find everything you need to create an environment in your household, classroom, ball field – or anywhere for that matter – to empower young people to pursue love and good deeds first and, through first-hand experiences, teach them the power and concept of "when we give, we receive."

The birth of *Dollars of Love* occurred one sunny Florida afternoon when Elaine and I were profoundly moved by the verse Luke 12:34: "For where your treasure is there your heart will be also." It challenged us to really evaluate ourselves as parents in what we were teaching our children to focus on and what they should treasure.

From the time we are born, society slams down our throats that children need to pursue accolades and financial success; we are taught that these are life's most important treasures. Children start school, where good grades are treasured and winning awards are the focal point for anything they do, and they treasure these trophies.

Our children are taught that good grades will lead to good colleges, and this, in turn, will result in a high-paying job where we can buy lots of things. To make matters worse, we make children perform chores for money so that they can buy things they treasure.

What sort of pathways in their brains are we creating at such a young age? In our opinion, these pathways lead to selfishness instead of selflessness. It also hinders the pursuit of their higher calling, instead taught to suppress it to focus on society's harmful, generalized concept of treasure.

We, as parents, decided that we did not want our children to grow up idolizing the treasures society tells us we need. They will have plenty of time to work and make money, but in our children's formidable years, we decided it was necessary to provide them with a foundation for pursuing love, kindness, and good deeds.

Thus, the birth of *Dollars of Love* – a currency available to all walks of life, regardless of socioeconomic status. Dollars of Love is the most powerful kind of currency because it is earned through performing good deeds and actions of love.

So, what, exactly, is a dollar of love? It is what your kids receive when they perform good deeds. At the end of the day, they will reflect upon each dollar of love earned and write on the back of it how it made them feel. At the end of the week, they can turn their dollars of love in for a prize.

In the beginning, the prizes will reinforce their positive behavior, but as the weeks progress, the children will realize that the action of love earning them the dollar of love made them feel better than any prize they were awarded. This creates a pathway where it becomes second nature for the child to perform a good deed. It becomes a part of who they are.

We also inadvertently came across the concept of saving the dollars of love and trading them for rewards of various sizes. This taught our children patience and fiscal responsibility, which are important later in life.

Bryson and Brady were fast asleep when they were suddenly awoken to the familiar song from Sam the ice cream truck outside.

3

The boys quickly ran to their piggy bank so that they could buy some ice cream — just like the other boys and girls in the neighborhood. But when they got to their piggy bank, Bryson and Brady were shocked to find their bank was empty!

The brothers looked on from their bedroom window as all the kids in the neighborhood bought their favorite ice creams.

7

The boys walked downstairs with tears in their eyes and big frowns on their faces.

"What's wrong, boys? Why the long faces?" Their Mom and Dad asked.

Bryson replied, "ALL the other boys and girls have money to buy ice cream. But we don't have any money!"

"We're too poor to buy anything!" Brady cried.

The boy's dad smiled and said, "So, boys, you want to be rich?"
Bryson and Brady smiled widely and quickly replied, "Yes! We want to be rich like the other kids."
Mom told the boys, "To be rich, you have to know what wealth really means."

11

Dad said, "We want you to understand that helping others is what will make you rich." He pulled out a big piece of paper that had colorful lines all over it.

"Take this treasure map," he told Bryson and Brady. "It will lead you to riches!"

Mom added, "Every time you help others and perform a good deed today, you will receive a dollar of love."

13

"What's a dollar of Love?" the boys
asked.
Mom held a bill out for Bryson and
Brady to take.
"This dollar of Love is the most
powerful kind of currency, because it's
a symbol of your kindness and that
you are loving and caring people."
"Work hard to perform as many good
deeds as possible and fill your piggy
banks with dollars of Love!"

Bryson and Brady took off running, the dollars of Love map in hand. The boys' first stop on their treasure map was to go to the beach. The clue said they had to make the whole world beautiful.

When Bryson and Brady arrived, they noticed that the beach was so dirty that the animals were becoming sick!
The boys decided to help the world by picking up all the trash on the sand.
"ALL done, now on to the next clue!" said Brady once they had finished.

19

Next on the treasure map was that the boys needed to help thirsty people. Picking up the trash was hard, and so Bryson and Brady decided to share their mom's famous ice-cold lemonade with the hardworking garbagemen of the neighborhood.
As the boys gave lemonade to their new friends, they saw their elderly neighbor Ms.Smith trying to clean up fallen leaves in her yard.

21

Bryson and Brady quickly ran over to her house to pick up all the leaves. Little did the boys know that helping a friend in need was a clue on their treasure map!

The boys were tired from all their hard work and wanted to sit down in the park and rest. Bryson noticed a boy from summer camp sitting all alone after being bullied. Brady decided that this would be a perfect place to sit and tell their friend that he is great.

Next, Bryson and Brady's treasure map said that they needed to help the injured or sick. As they thought about how to do this, they heard a baby bird crying and wanting to get back in its nest.

The boys were both excellent tree climbers and had no trouble putting the bird back with its brothers and sisters inside the nest.

Brady looked at Bryson and said, "These weak trees are not strong enough to be a bird's home." Bryson agreed, and the boys decided to plant another tree that could grow into a strong shelter for their bird friends.

The boys had just completed their next clue on the treasure map — giving shelter to those in need!

The two boys looked at their treasure map. Next, they needed to provide food for the hungry. They walked to the market to get some tasty things for the meal. Suddenly, Bryson and Brady saw a worker drop all his cans on the floor!
People walked by, laughing at the man. The boys quickly jumped into action and picked up the cans. The worker was so thankful!

With their delicious food in their hands, Bryson and Brady headed to the next stop on the treasure map — their church. The boys prepared food and then gave some to every hungry person at the church.

Brady told Bryson, "The treasure map says that we need to use our talents to brighten someone's day." Bryson said, "We can go to grandma's group home and make the residents smile with singing and dancing!"
And so the boys ran to their grandma's and danced and sang their favorite songs. They made all the center's residents laugh and smile!

35

As Bryson and Brady left their grandma's group home, they saw a hardworking police officer trying to get rid of mean words on the walls. The boys knew straight away that this was a perfect way to finish the next clue on their treasure map — turning something bad into something good and beautiful. So, they grabbed a paintbrush and began to help paint the walls.

It was getting dark, so Bryson and Brady started walking home. On their way, they saw their friend, T.J., on the baseball diamond. He looked very upset!

Bryson asked T.J. what he was so sad about. "I do not know how to play!" he cried.

Brady smiled at T.J. and said, "It's okay! We can help you learn how to play!"

All three boys began playing baseball. Soon, Bryson and Brady had helped their friend learn how to hit the ball farther than anyone else in school!

Bryson and Brady finally arrived home to their mom and dad.
"How did your day go?" Mom asked.
The boys smiled and told their parents that they had earned ten dollars of love! They explained to their parents that the feeling of helping others, was far better than anything money could ever buy!

Mom said, "We are so proud of you both! Today you learned the true meaning of wealth. Now, would you like to turn in those hard-earned dollars of love for a prize?"

The boys jumped up and down gleefully and said, "We would love an ice cream party!"

Dad said, "We thought you would ask for that! Go into the backyard and claim your prize."

Bryson and Brady quickly ran into the backyard. Everyone they had helped today was waiting for them! Each person had a tub of ice cream in their hands. There were chocolate, vanilla, strawberry, and even cotton candy flavors!

Bryson and Brady, their mom and dad, and everyone from the neighborhood all sat enjoying their ice creams.

The boys' dad told them, "Today, you have learned the message that when we give we will receive."

Their mom said, "Any act of love is worth more than money. Love makes us the richest humans on Earth and when we help others it makes us feel so happy!"

Bryson and Brady smiled and said " Yes! These dollars of love remind us to always try our best to help make the whole world beautiful!"

The End

Bryson and Brady earned dollars of Love!

You can start earning your Dollars of Love today!!

49

DoLLars of Love

The whole World is Beautiful

DoLLars of Love

The whole World is Beautiful

DoLLars of Love

The whole World is Beautiful

DoLLars of Love

The whole World is Beautiful

Dollars of Love

The whole World is Beautiful

Dollars of Love

The whole World is Beautiful

DoLLars of Love

The whole World is Beautiful

DoLLars of Love

The whole World is Beautiful

Made in the USA
Las Vegas, NV
01 December 2021

35775476R00040

This is the story of two brothers, Bryson and Brady, who are too poor to buy ice cream like the other boys and girls in their neighborhood. Bryson and Brady want nothing more in life than to be rich so that they can buy anything their hearts desire.

The boys' parents worry that Bryson and Brady do not realize what it means to be rich, so they send them on a treasure hunt, focused on performing good deeds.

As Bryson and Brady perform these acts of kindness, they earn something called 'Dollars of Love.' These Dollars of Love teach Bryson and Brady the true definition of wealth. As the boys earn more and more Dollars of Love, they begin to realize that, through actions of love and kindness, they gain something far more valuable than money could ever buy.

At the end of their treasure hunt, Bryson and Brady are rich with Dollars of Love and turn them in for a wonderful prize with all the friends they made along the way.

$11.99
ISBN 978-1-7379934-4-5
51199>

9 781737 993445